SCIENCE IN VIEW T

MATERIALS

JACK FIELDHOUSE

STUART ROBERTSON

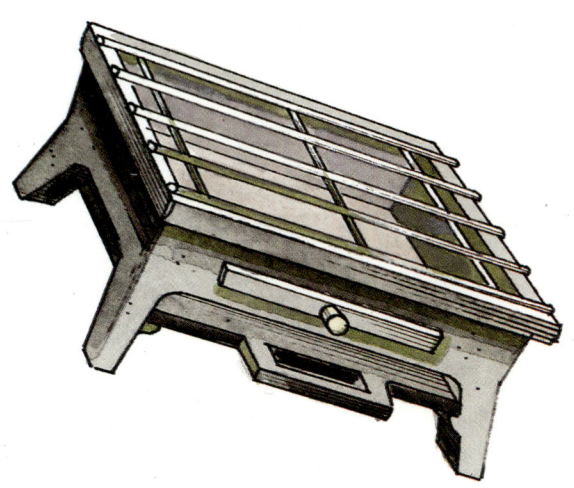

Oxford University Press

Oxford University Press, Walton Street, Oxford OX2 6 DP

Oxford New York Toronto
Delhi Bombay Calcutta Madras Karachi
Petaling Jaya Singapore Hong Kong Tokyo
Nairobi Dar es Salaam Cape Town
Melbourne Auckland

and associated companies in
Berlin Ibadan

Oxford is a trade mark of Oxford University Press

© Jack Fieldhouse, Stuart Robertson, 1986

Reissued as module, 1989

ISBN 0 19 914309 9

Acknowledgements

The publishers would like to thank the following for permission to reproduce transparencies:

Ashmolean Museum, Oxford: p.6; Austin Rover: p.5 (top); Barnaby's Picture Library: p.12 (bottom), p.21; British Railways Board: p.5 (top); Cement and Concrete Association: p.7; Central Electricity Generating Board: p.12 (middle); Civil Aviation Authority: p.26 (top); John Cleare: p.5 (2nd from bottom), p.13 (top); Richard Costain Limited: p.5 (top); John Dawkins: p.5 (top), p.16, p.19; Peter Fletcher: p.9 (2nd from bottom), p.29 (bottom left); Forestry commission: p.14 (right); Fothergill and Harvey plc: p.5 (second from top); Alex Fraser: p.5, p.9 (middle left); Terry Jennings: p.22 (bottom); Mansell Collection: p.15, p.23 (top and bottom); Press Association: p.22 (top); Rentokill Limited: p.29 (top); Science Photo Library: p.12 (top), p.13 (bottom); Shirley Institute: p.10; Adrian Smith: p.31 (top); Topham Picture Library: p.30 (middle).

Cover pictures: photography by Chris Honeywell; illustrations by Ben Manchipp

Illustrated by: Ed McLachlan Ben Manchipp Colin Meier Oxford Illustrators Peter Russell Martin Salisbury Paul Thomas

Photography by: Chris Honeywell

Photographic props loaned by: Boswells, Oxford; J.W. Carpenter Ltd.; C.J. Heating Ltd., Oxford.

Our special thanks to: The Civil Aviation Fire Training School, Darlington and Fire Service College, Moreton-in-Marsh for setting fire to things.

Printed in Hong Kong

Introduction

This book has been written to support one core topic in the Scottish Standard Grade Science Course. It should also be a valuable asset for many GCSE science courses, as it recognizes the importance of students' own experiences and interests.

This book is organized in double-page spreads which can be used as the basis for a lesson. Experimental details and results are used extensively for development of information-handling and problem-solving skills. The experiments described could form the starting point for students' practical investigations. However, class practical work has purposely not been given. This will allow the teacher the freedom to select the practical back-up most appropriate to the interests of the students and resources available. The book is fully illustrated and comprehensively indexed.

Each double-page spread contains a variety of questions which allow students to develop skills in obtaining and presenting information, carrying out calculations, suggesting and describing experimental procedures, drawing conclusions, and making predictions. These questions are also valuable for the assessment of these skills and could be used to build up a profile of the student's progress.

The book contains a thorough coverage of the specific Standard Grade objectives in knowledge and understanding relating to the 'Materials' topic. The text has also been designed to develop the skills of handling information and problem-solving.

Questions have been colour coded to correspond to three levels of performance: most pupils should be successful with questions coded with yellow; blue codes represent a greater challenge; and red codes require a relatively high level of performance.

Contents

Looking at materials	4
The variety of uses	5
The magic of mixing	6
Hard facts	7
Dressing up	8
Properties of materials	9
Checking out materials	10
Putting it into practice	11
The right one for the job	12
Fibres	13
Choosing materials	14
Keeping dry	15
Iron and steel	16
Strong steel	17
Plastic	18
Rubber	19
Strength and shape	20
Even stronger	21
Flammability	22
Lavoiser	23
Dangerous stuff	24
Avoiding danger	25
Fire hazard	26
Poisonous gases	27
Damage and protection	28
Dry rot	29
Metal corrosion	30
Protection against corrosion	31

Looking at materials

Sorting out materials

Human beings are very good at making use of their surroundings. Early people used natural materials like stone and wood for making tools and weapons. They used caves for shelter and protection, and used animal skins for clothing. As time went by people learnt to make weapons and tools from metals. They built houses from stone, brick, and wood and wove cloth to make clothes. Today we can even make and use totally new materials such as nylon. These new materials are called **man-made materials**

1 In the diagram you can see a variety of objects made from different materials. Arrange them into two lists according to whether they are made from natural or man-made materials.

Natural and man-made materials

Why classify?

There are many ways of grouping materials. One way is according to their use. For example, materials can be used for **clothes** or for **shelter**. The **properties** of a material are the things it can do. For example, one property of glass is that it lets light through. Materials are often grouped according to their properties.

Knowing what group a material belongs to can tell us what to expect about its properties. For example, if an unknown material can be placed in the group 'metals' because of its hardness and appearance, then we would expect it to conduct electricity because all metals conduct electricity.

2 Copy the two lists of materials (on the right) and complete them by adding a heading to each group.

3 A mystery material is found on the moon. It is hard and rough and conducts electricity. Use the table shown to identify which group the material belongs to and list its properties.

copper	plastic
aluminium	nylon
iron	wood
zinc	paper
steel	stone

Supply the missing headings

property	group A	group B	group C
lets light through	yes	no	yes
hardness	very hard	hard	soft
appearance	smooth	rough	smooth
conducts electricity	no	yes	no
dissolves in water	no	yes	no

Which group does the mystery material belong to?

The variety of uses

Uses of steel

Uses of copper

Uses of nylon

Uses of polystyrene

Many uses for the same material

Materials can be used to make lots of different things.

Strong, tough steel probably has the largest number of uses ranging from small objects such as paper clips to large steel beams used in building.

Copper is a beautiful and a useful metal. It is an excellent conductor of electricity and so is used for making wires, cables, and other electrical parts. Copper can also conduct heat well. This explains why pipes, boilers, and cooking pots are often made of copper.

When nylon was first manufactured in the mid-1930s it was used mainly to make ladies stockings which came to be called 'nylons'. Nowadays it has many more uses.

Polystyrene is a type of plastic. Its uses include model kits, disposable cups, and various types of packaging.

1 Use the photographs to list some uses of steel, copper, nylon, and polystyrene.

2 List as many different materials as you can which are used for:
   a cooking pots
   b clothing
   c building houses
   d packaging.

3 Suggest why steel frying pans often have copper bottoms.

The magic of mixing

Metal magic

Copper has been used by man for almost 10 000 years. At first people probably found lumps of copper lying on the ground and hammered them into the shape they wanted. However, we don't usually find pure copper. It is usually found in the ground joined with other substances. This is called a copper **ore**.

About 7000 years ago man discovered how to separate pure copper from its ores by using heat. Separating a metal from its ore in this way is called **smelting**. People were able to use pure copper to make tools, ornaments, and vessels but there was one big snag! Copper, like many pure metals is soft. It *pulls* apart if you stretch it and, what is more important, it can't be used to make a cutting edge. A copper knife is useless!

A remarkable discovery was made in the Middle East about 6000 years ago. By mixing a little tin with the molten copper a new substance called **bronze** could be made. Bronze was much harder than copper and could be used for making cutting edges. A metal mixed with another substance is called an **alloy**. Bronze is an alloy of tin and copper.

This discovery must have astonished those who made it since tin is even softer than copper. Yet mixed together they made this new hard substance. Nowadays we know that the tin acts as a sort of grit, getting between the copper particles and stopping them from sliding apart when pulled.

The history of steel (an alloy of iron and carbon) is more recent than copper because it is more difficult to extract iron from its ores. It is thought that iron was widely used near the Black Sea about 3500 years ago and 500 years later people in India could make steel. Nowadays man has learnt to make a large number of different alloys. Some of them are shown in the table.

1 What is meant by an alloy?

2 What name is given to an alloy of:
  a copper and tin,
  b iron and carbon?

3 What is the main idea you have been reading about above?
  a Copper
  b Iron
  c Bronze
  d Steel
  e Alloys

4 Explain in your own words why mixing two soft metals together can produce a hard alloy.

5 Use books to find out all you can about alloys then copy and complete the table.

A food vessel, chinese bronze, 800 BC

Alloy	Made from	Uses
Steel	—	—
—	copper and tin	—
solder	—	electrical joints joining metals
—	magnesium and aluminium	atomic reactor fuel cans engine blocks
stainless steel	—	cutlery, sinks medical equipment
—	copper and zinc	—
pewter	tin and lead	—
cupro-nickel	—	copper coins

Alloys and their uses

Hard facts

Concrete, a modern material?

Concrete is another good example of how a hard wearing material can be made by mixing the right things together. Although concrete is often thought of as a modern material it was discovered by the Romans about 2000 years ago.

Concrete is a mixture of three things, cement, water, and aggregate. Aggregate is a gritty material like sand or small stones. Cement when mixed with water forms a stone-like 'glue' which binds together the particles of aggregate to make them strong.

The strength of concrete depends on several things. One important thing is the amount of water added to the mixture. Only a small amount is needed to harden the cement. Any extra water has to evaporate (dry up). This leaves small holes in the concrete and makes it weak.

The strength of concrete also depends on which aggregate is used. A coarse aggregate such as crushed stone has sharp particles. This produces a strong concrete but is hard to mix. A fine aggregate such as sand has smooth round particles. This produces a weak concrete, usually called mortar, which is easy to mix and can be used for brick laying. Usually the aggregate used for concrete is a mixture of sand and stone. The *right* mixture of sand and stone makes a very strong concrete.

Crushed stone — a coarse aggregate

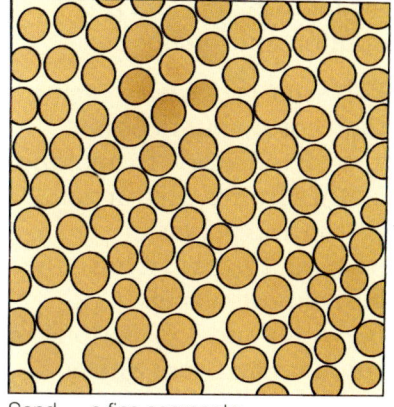

Sand — a fine aggregate

1 What 3 things are mixed to make concrete?

2 Name two things which decide the strength of concrete.

3 How is mortar made and what is it used for?

In an experiment 7 samples of concrete were made by mixing different amounts of cement, fine aggregate, and coarse aggregate. The samples were then tested for strength on a special machine. The results are given in the graph. On this graph 1:1:6 means 1 part of cement mixed with 1 part fine aggregate and 6 parts of coarse aggregate.

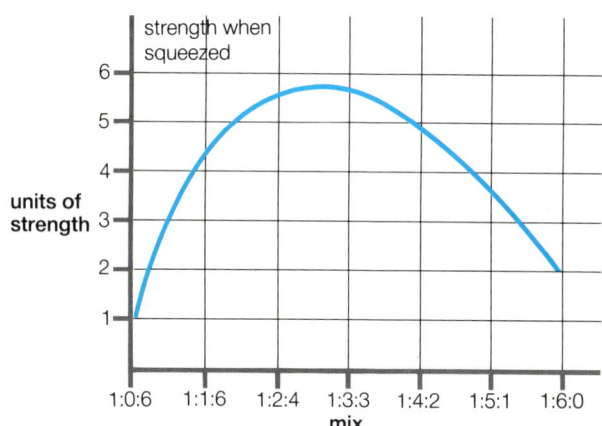

A graph showing how the strength of concrete depends on the mixture

4 Which mixture is the weakest?

5 Which mixture is the strongest?

6 If you had 2 bags of cement and you wished to use them both to mix up some of the strongest mixture how many bags of sand and how many bags of coarse aggregate would you need?

Dressing up

The best of both worlds

Clothes can be made from a wide variety of materials: **natural fibres** such as cotton or wool, **man-made fibres**, such as nylon or polyester, or a mixture of fibres. A **fibre** is a long thin thread of material, like a hair. The label on a piece of clothing usually tells you about the material used. Cotton absorbs moisture and allows sweat to evaporate. It is comfortable on hot days.

Polyester is harder wearing than cotton but does not absorb moisture. By making clothes from a mixture of cotton and polyester manufacturers can have the best of both worlds. 65% polyester and 35% cotton is a common mixture. Shirts made from this are hard wearing, comfortable in Summer and drip-dry.

A man-made fibre or mixture may be made by many different companies and sold under different **trade** or **brand names**.

1 Which of the following are natural fibres: wool, cotton, nylon, polyester?

2 Name a natural fibre which comes from a plant.

3 Give a brand name for a wool/cotton mixture.

4 Give the brand name of one man-made fibre which is made from chemicals coming from oil.

5 How does a pure cotton shirt differ from one made from 65% polyester: 35% cotton?

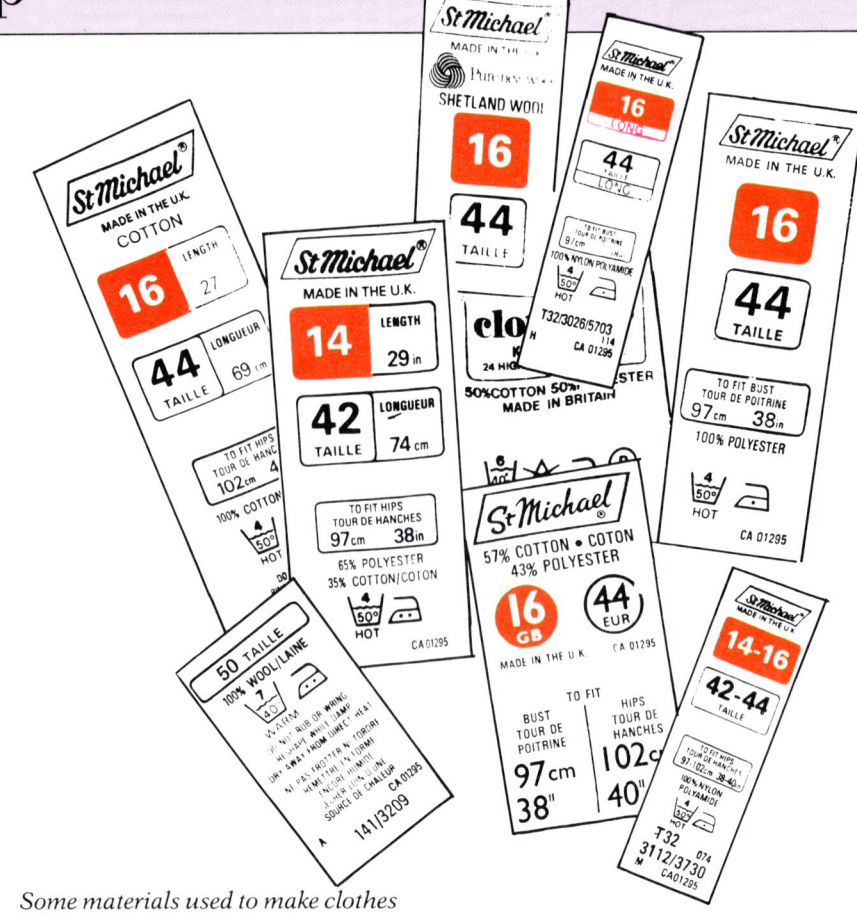

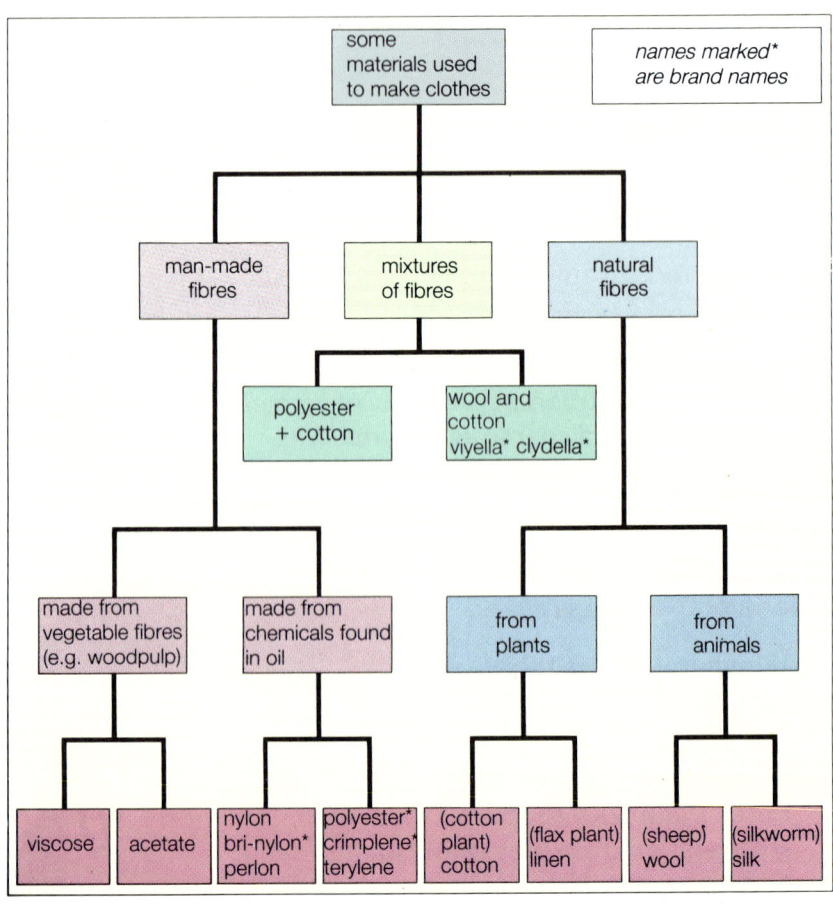

Some materials used to make clothes

A key showing some of the fibres used to make clothes and their brand names

Properties of materials

Concrete

Formica

Glass

PVC

Stainless steel

Diamond

Useful properties

The properties of a material may include the way a material looks, feels, or behaves.

Strength is the ability not to change its shape when pulled, squeezed, or twisted. Steel and concrete are strong materials and are often used to support buildings.

Hardness is the ability to stand up to wear and scratches. Materials with this property are often needed to cut other less hard materials. Diamond is the hardest of all natural materials.

Resisting water or being **waterproof** is a useful property of materials like rubber and PVC.

Materials which are **heat-resistant** can often be found on kitchen work surfaces where hot objects are placed. However, pots and pans are made from metals having exactly the opposite property. These are chosen to let heat through easily. This is the property of being a **good conductor** of heat.

1 Make a list of as many materials as you can used in the home and opposite each write two of its properties.

2 Give as many examples as you can of a hard materials being used to cut a softer material.

3 What properties are shown in the photographs?

9

Checking out materials

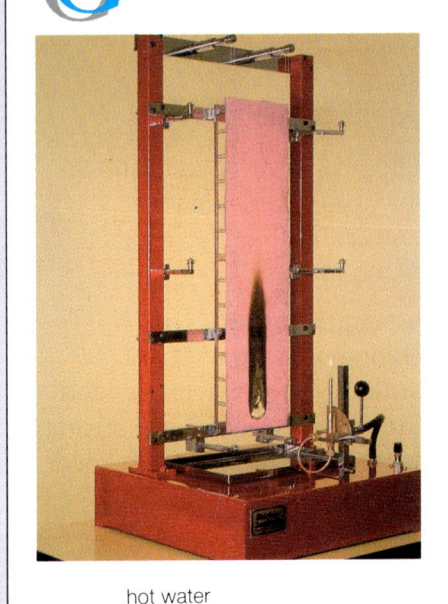

Flame testing a fabric

A **flammable** fabric continues to burn after the flame which set it alight has been removed. A **flameproof** fabric does not catch fire or goes out very quickly.

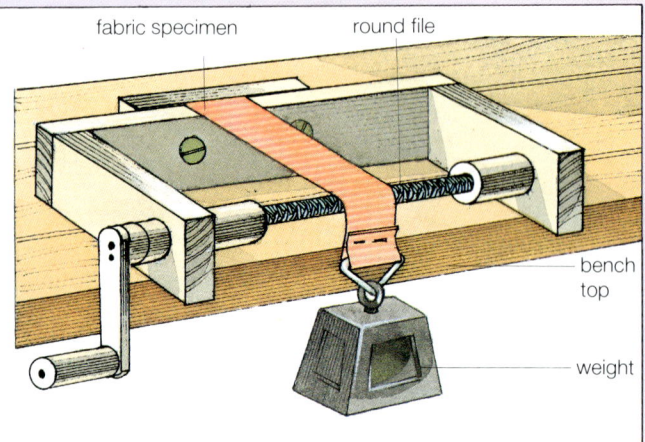

Comparing the thermal conductivity of aluminium, brass, and iron

Thermal conductivity

The **thermal conductivity** of a material is a measure of how easily it allows heat to pass through it. This apparatus is comparing the thermal conductivity of bars of iron, brass, and aluminium.

Mystery test

In this test wire made from different metals is being compared. In each case the number of weights needed to snap the wire is recorded.

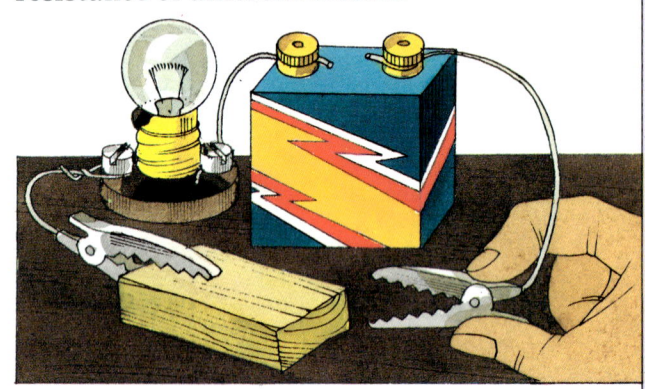

Wear resistance of a fabric

The handle in the diagram is turned until a hole is worn in the fabric. Using such an apparatus it is possible to compare the **wear resistance** of different fabrics.

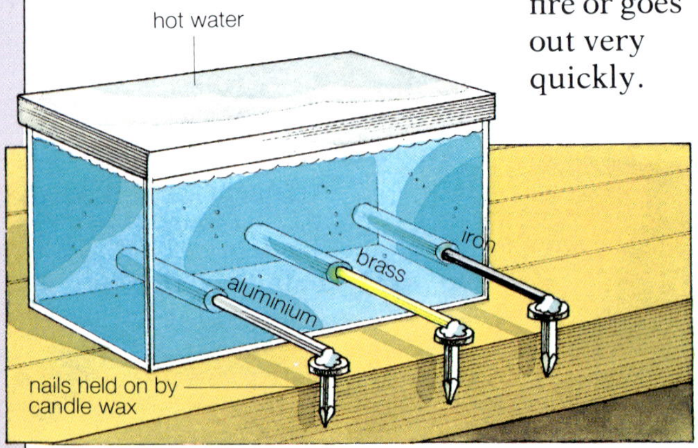

Electrical conductivity

A material with good **electrical conductivity** allows electricity to pass through it easily. If the bulb in the diagram lights the material is a **good conductor** of electricity. If it does not light it is a bad conductor or **insulator**.

1 Give a reason for flame testing a fabric.

2 a Describe how to carry out an experiment to compare the wear resistance of nylon and cotton.
  b How would you make sure it was a fair test?

3 Explain how the apparatus shown can be used to compare thermal conductivity.

4 What property is being compared in the mystery test? Describe the experimental procedure.

5 Why would it be difficult to *compare* the electrical conductivity of three different metals using the electrical conductivity apparatus.

Putting it into practice

Teapot trouble

J.G. Wood, a manufacturer of household goods, wants to make and sell a teapot mat designed to stop hot teapots burning table surfaces. Wood instructs D. Baker, his head of research, to test three different materials to see which is the most suitable. The research department uses the apparatus shown on the previous page but changes it slightly by adding three identical thermometers. After the tests Baker presents Wood with the results shown in the graph and table. However, due to the rush, one set of results has been missed out of the graph and none of the lines have been labelled. Can you sort out the confusion and save Baker's skin?

1. Redraw the apparatus used to measure thermal conductively showing where the three thermometers were added.
2. Which result did Baker miss out?
3. According to the results which material should Wood choose?
4. Copy the graph and complete it by adding the line showing the missing result.

A sticky problem

Mr Baker next tackles the problem of finding the strongest glue to stick on the feet of the mat. His apparatus and results are shown opposite.

5. Describe in your own words how he did the experiment.
6. What is the strongest glue?
7. Although they seem to be the same describe how you could test to see if Nevastick was stronger than Upstick?
8. What other properties should Baker test the glues for?
9. Imagine you are Baker. Write a report to Wood describing your results. You may use diagrams and graphs in the report. Finish the report by telling Wood how the teapot mat should be made.

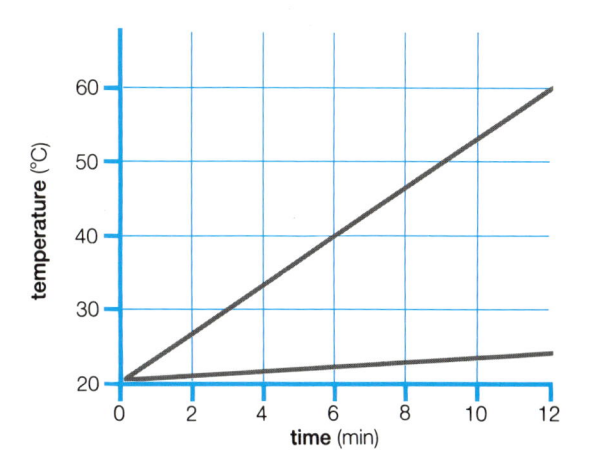

time (min)	temperature (°C)		
	copper	brass	glass
0	20	20	20
1	23.2	21.5	20.4
2	26.4	22.8	20.9
3	30	24	21.2
4	33.2	25.2	21.3
5	36.5	26.4	21.7
6	39.8	28	22
7	43.2	29.1	22.3
8	46.4	30.5	22.6
9	50	32	22.9
10	53.2	33.2	23.2
11	56.4	34.6	23.6
12	60	36	24

D. Baker's results shown as a table

	aha	neva stick	pratt	up stick
kg weights to break joint	1	3	4	3

Glue testing and results

The right one for the job

Metals

Metals are good conductors of electricity and have many uses in industry for carrying both small and large electric currents. You can see in the photograph how aluminium is used to connect the different parts of a circuit on a silicon chip. The photograph shows transmission cables carrying electricity across the country.

Metals can also be very strong. The steel wires used to build suspension bridges such as the one shown can be pulled by great forces without breaking. This type of steel is called **high-tensile** steel.

Plastic

Although not as strong as steel, plastic is a very useful material. It is light, hard wearing, does not rot, is a good insulator of heat as well as electricity, and it can be attractively coloured. Many different types of plastic such as PVC, clear polystyrene, expanded polystyrene, phenolic resin, and nylon can be found around the home.

1 Give an example of a metal being used because it is a good conductor of electricity.

2 Give an example of a metal being used because it is very strong.

3 List as many different plastic objects as you can in the room shown below.

4 List the property of the plastic which makes it suitable for each use.

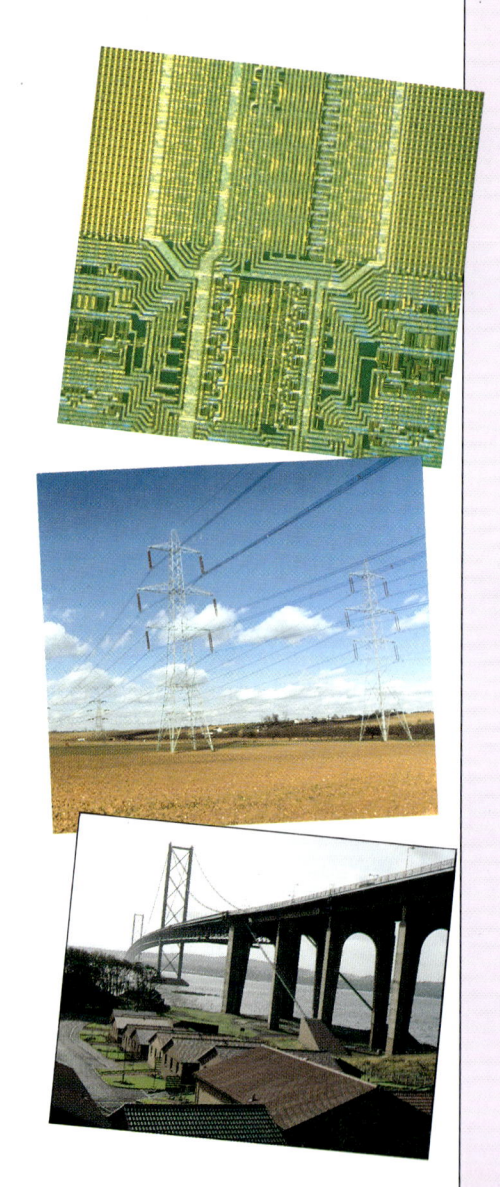

Fibres

Fibres and fabrics

Although a single fibre is not very strong a bundle of fibres can be twisted together to make a rope. Ropes made from nylon fibres are both strong and lightweight and are very useful to mountaineers.

Fibres can also be made into a **fabric** or cloth. Clothes are made from fabric because it is attractive, flexible, and warm. Fabrics keep us warm because they trap air between the fibres. Air is a good insulator of heat. Notice that the insulating property of fabrics does not depend on the fibre but how the fabric is made. The thicker the fabric the more air is trapped and the warmer it keeps us. A knitted fibre has gaps in it which allow air through to carry away body heat. A woven fibre does not do this so easily and so it is warmer than a knitted fibre.

Glass fibres

Glass is amazing stuff! Used as a window it is solid to keep out the wind and rain yet it lets through the sunshine to warm and cheer our homes.

By drawing out the molten glass during its making, glass can even be made into long flexible fibres. A beam of light will bounce along inside one of these fibres even though the fibre bends. This has led to the exciting invention of **fibre optics**. A cable made from bundles of these glass fibres can be made to carry thousands of telephone messages at the same time. This is done by using very strong light from a laser and chopping up the light beam to send the messages in code.

1 Explain why mountaineers find nylon ropes useful.

2 Which is best used for an overcoat, a knitted or a woven fabric? Explain your answer.

3 Explain why some fabrics are warmer than others.

4 Find out one other use than for telephone cables of optical fibres and write a short note about it.

A nylon rope

Knitted fabric

Woven fabric

Fibre optic cables use light to carry thousands of telephone conversations at the same time

Choosing materials

Choosing materials

Why choose that?

The properties of a material are not the only things to be considered when deciding whether to use it for a job.

Cost

Aluminium does not rust like steel. So why aren't all cars made of aluminium? A glance at the graph gives us the answer. It would cost too much!

Availability

The builder of the log cabin shown would have been very foolish to use brick and mortar when there was so much wood readily available.

Appearance

Velvet is sometimes chosen for curtains because of its rich warm appearance. However it is expensive!

Health

The use of certain materials is sometimes unhealthy. Although asbestos is an excellent fire-proof material it has recently been found that the fibres from some sorts of asbestos can cause cancer.

Safety

Expanded polystyrene tiles look nice and help stop heat escaping through the ceiling. However, in a fire they melt and drip burning pieces into the room which spreads the fire. For safety reasons it is best not to use them.

1 List 6 things which affect choice of materials.

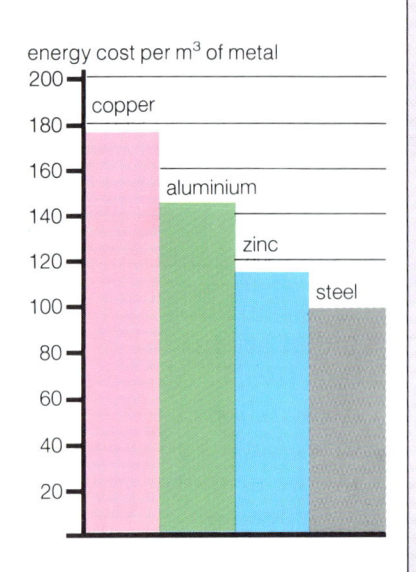

Velvet curtains look attractive but are expensive

Log cabins are built in areas where there is plenty of wood

energy cost per m³ of metal (copper, aluminium, zinc, steel)

ASBESTOS COMMITTEE POINTS TO WORKMEN'S CANCER TOLL

By Tom Forest

SIXTY-ONE workmen who were employed in building Glasgow's asbestos-ridden Red Road flats have since died — 52 of cancer.

The pressure group Clydeside Action on Asbestos has traced 180 workers who were involved in building the multi-storey flats in the 1960s. The group was not surprised to find that 60 of those identified have died over the past 20 years but it was alarmed to learn that 52 had died from cancer, which is three times the average figure.

Keeping dry

Singing in the rain

My name is Charles Macintosh and until recently I ran a cloth-dyeing business in Glasgow. One of the jobs that we cloth-dyers hate doing is cleaning the dye off the machines. So, imagine my delight when, six years ago in 1819, I heard that naphtha cleans off the dye beautifully. Naphtha, or coal oil, is one of the things left over when coal is heated to make coal-gas. The new coal-gas companies springing up all over didn't know what to do with the stuff and were throwing it away. Smelling a bargain, I bought a quantity very cheaply from the Glasgow Gas Works to try out. And then came my stroke of luck! While cleaning some machines in the workshop, I made the remarkable discovery that naphtha dissolves rubber. When I spread the sticky solution on the table the naphtha soon dried out leaving a thin coat of rubber. Then I had the brilliant idea of spreading some of this 'liquid rubber' onto a sheet of cotton and when it had dried I found that water could hardly pass through the cotton. I then tried pressing two sheets together as I have shown in the drawing. Success! I had invented a new flexible, water-proof material.

It wasn't long before I was selling 'the new Macintosh' waterproof cape. Although it is selling really well now, at first it was criticised very heavily by doctors. They said that although it stopped rain getting in it also stopped sweat getting out and so it was very unhealthy. I think they were angry that fewer people were catching colds.

Charles Macintosh

This is how Macintosh made his waterproof material

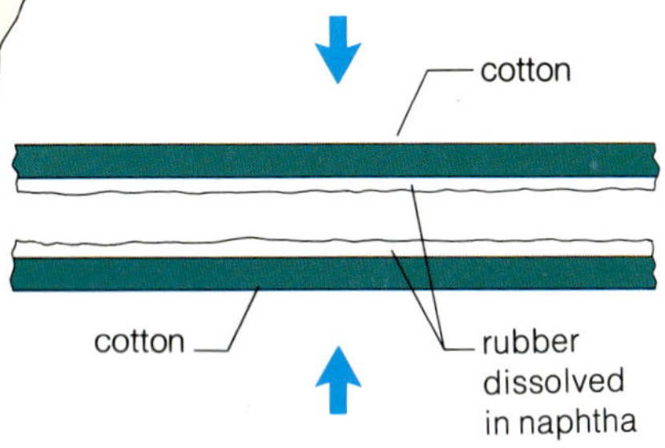

The first waterproof garment the macintosh

1 What is the above mainly about?
 a The discovery of Naphtha.
 b Cloth dying.
 c The discovery of rubber.
 d The discovery of a waterproof material.

2 Where does the chemical naphtha come from?

3 In what year was this written?

4 What important discovery did Macintosh make which enabled him to invent the new water-proof material?

5 What piece of clothing is still named after Macintosh?

6 Explain in your own words how far Macintosh's choice of materials for his new discovery was affected by properties, costs, availability, appearance, health, and safety. Write a sentence about each.

Iron and steel

Iron

Iron is an **element** or pure substance which is usually found in the ground mixed with earth, rocks, and other impurities. This mixture of substances is called **iron ore**. To separate the iron from the other substances, the ore must be heated in a **smelting furnace**. In this type of furnace the iron ore is mixed with a fuel which draws off the impurities from the iron as it burns.

Some furnaces remove almost all the impurities and leave behind a very pure iron called **wrought iron**. This is soft and easily hammered into different shapes. Two red-hot pieces hammered together become tightly joined so this iron is often used to make ornamental gates. However, it is too soft and easily worn away to be used for supporting heavy loads.

By melting iron ore in a different type of furnace and allowing it to mix with some **carbon** a much stronger type of iron called **cast iron** can be made. This iron can be poured while still hot into moulds and so formed into different shapes. Although it is hard, cast iron is also very brittle and it does not stand up to sudden shocks. It is useful for making, among other things, man-hole covers and garden rollers, and it was once used for making drain pipes.

Wrought iron

Cast iron

Steel

Wrought iron contains almost no carbon and cast iron contains up to 4.5% carbon.

Steel is the name given to any alloy of iron and carbon which contains between 0.25% and 4.5% carbon. The bar chart shows the percentage of carbon contained in the main types of iron and steel.

1 What is very pure iron called?

2 Which contains most carbon: a cast-iron lamp-post or a train rail made from medium carbon steel?

3 The steel in an axe-head contains 1% carbon. What kind of steel is it?

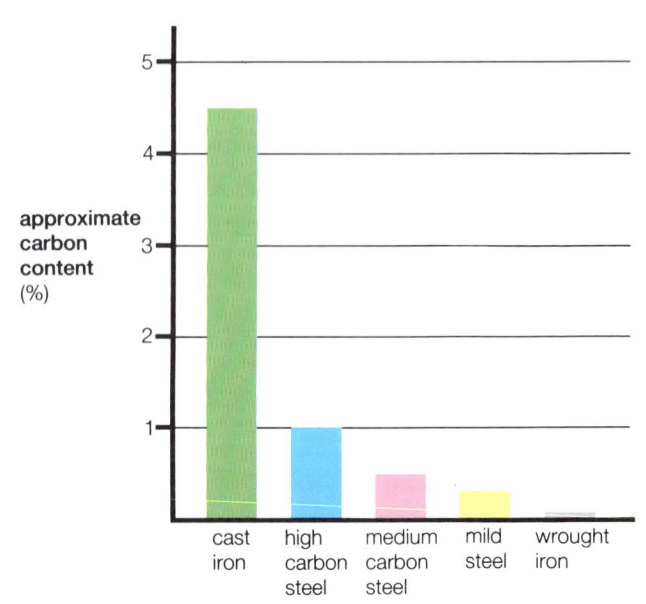

Carbon content of various iron alloys

Strong steel

Strong steel

The tensile strength of steel

The strength of a material can be measured by trying to pull it apart using a special machine. The force needed to break a piece of the material 1 square metre in area is called the **tensile strength** or simply **strength** of the material.

The graph shows how the strength of steel depends on the small amount of carbon contained in the iron. Use this and the bar chart on the previous page to answer the questions.

1 Arrange high carbon steel, mild steel, and medium steel in order of strength.

2 Which type of **steel** would you choose to make the support cables of a suspension bridge?

3 What is the tensile strength of wrought iron?

4 Use the information on page 16 to copy and extend the tensile strength graph to find out if cast iron is stronger than wrought iron.

Tensile strength is the force needed to break a piece of material whose cross-section is 1 m^3

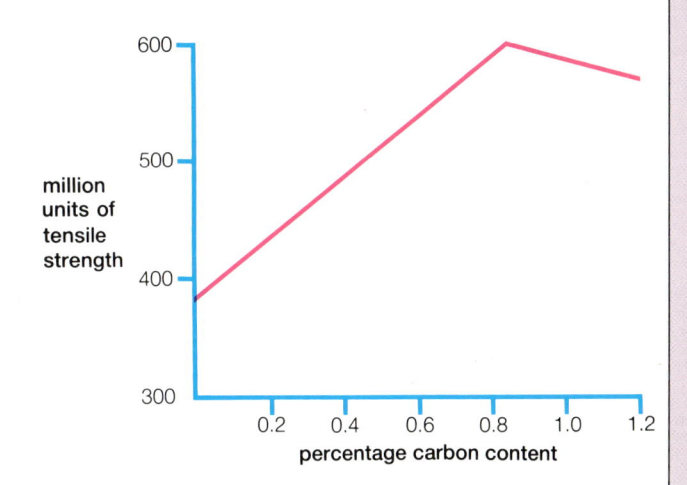

How the strength of steel is affected by the amount of carbon in the steel

Steel plus

The properties of steel can also be changed by adding small quantities of other metals while it is being made. 35% nickel added to a low-carbon steel produces an alloy called **invar**. This alloy is unusual because, unlike most metals, invar does not expand when it gets hot. Invar is used to make things which need to stay the same length even if they heat up. An example of this is a surveyor's long measuring tape.

Steel made with 1% carbon and 1.4% chromium is very hard and is used for making ball bearings.

Perhaps the best-known steel is **stainless steel** which is made from iron, 18% chromium and 8% nickel. This steel is sometimes called 18-8 stainless steel and is used to make things which must not rust.

5 Name three household objects which are made from stainless steel.

Stainless steel

Plastic

Plastic

Plastic is a name given to a whole family of man-made materials. Most plastics are made from chemicals found in oil although a few are made from other materials. Cellulose acetate for example is made from wood. Opposite is a list of some plastics. When most raw plastics are heated they become soft or 'plastic' and can be shaped into useful objects. This property gives the whole family of materials the name 'plastic' although each type of plastic has its own special name too.

All plastics are **polymers**. This means they have been made by forcing chemicals to join together to form long chains of molecules. Ethene molecules can be made to link together in long chains to form polythene. Styrene molecules linked together form polystyrene and so on. The word 'poly' means many. Plastics are made from long chains containing **many** molecules.

polythene	melamine resin
polystyrene	polyester resin
phenolic resin	polypropylene
polytetra-fluoroethene	nylon
	urea resin
polyvinyl-chloride	acrylic
	cellulose acetate

These are all types of plastic

1 List as many plastics as you can with names beginning with poly.

The effects of heat on plastics

Plastics which can be softened by heat are called **thermoplastics**. Plastics which cannot be softened by heat are called **thermosets**.

Use the key to help you answer the questions.

2 Which statement is true?
  a Most plastics come from oil.
  b Most plastics come from materials other than oil.

3 State whether the following are made from a thermoset or a thermoplastic: a formica work top, a melamine cup, a polystyrene tile, a nylon curtain rail.

4 Why does very hot water make a polythene bag sag but has no effect on a polythene basin?

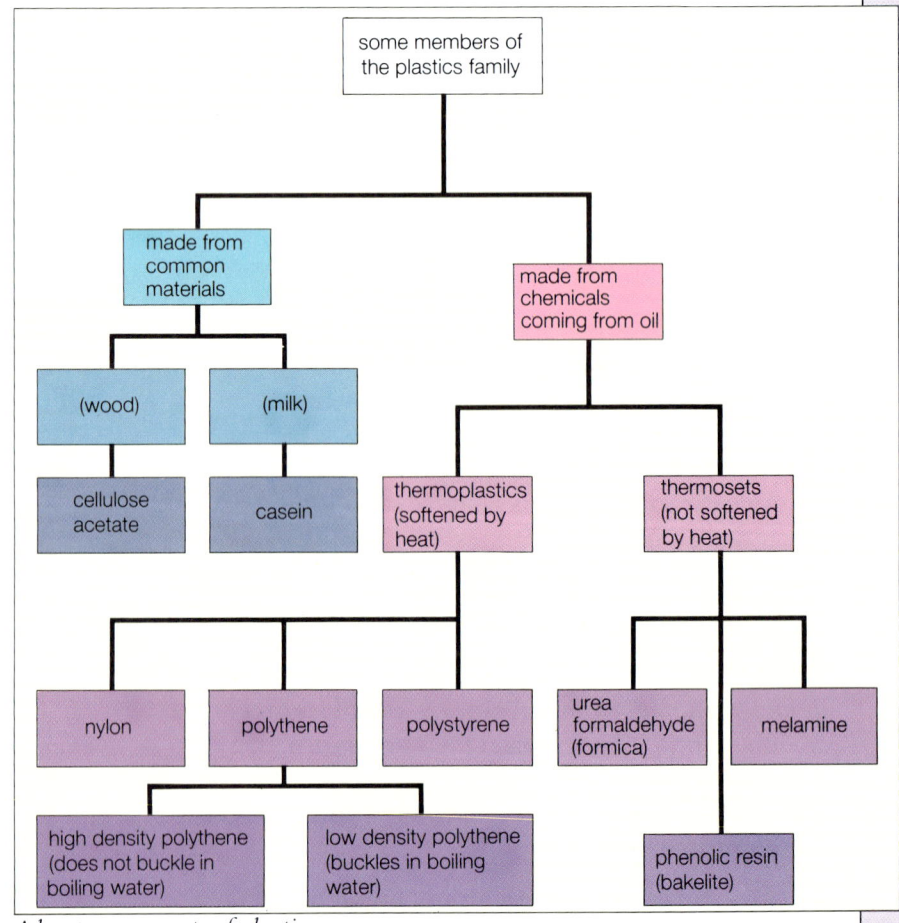

A key to some sorts of plastics

Rubber

What is rubber?

Like plastic, rubber is a polymer. However, it is neither a thermoset nor a thermoplastic. It is an **elastomer**. Rubber returns to its original shape when it is stretched and released. It behaves in an **elastic** way.

Raw rubber comes from **latex** which oozes out of the rubber tree once a groove has been cut in the bark. In its natural state rubber is not much good as it softens in heat and goes stiff in the cold. (Rather like a thermoplastic.) When rubber-coated shoes were first made in America, in the 1820s, people were disappointed to find that the shoes became soft in Summer and stiff in Winter. However, it was soon discovered that the natural properties of rubber could be changed by **vulcanization** that is, heating it with chemicals. This makes the rubber less likely to change with temperature.

Latex being collected from the rubber tree

Testing rubber

The information given is from the notebook of a scientist who works in the Bounco Rubber Company. She has been carrying out tests on different rubber samples and now must report back to her boss.

1 Use the scientist's results to calculate the *average* tensile strength of vulcanized and unvulcanized rubber.

2 Calculate the average hardness.

3 Copy and complete the table using the results from questions 1 and 2.

4 Imagine you are the scientist. Write a short report about the differences you have found between vulcanized and unvulcanized rubber.

A page from the scientist's notebook

4/11/86

Testing Rubber Samples

Sample	V or U	Property Measured	Result
1	V	T	32
2	U	T	43
3	V	T	3
4	V	T	34
5	U	H	4
6	U	H	22
7	V	H	38
8	V	T	30
9	U	T	29
10	V	H	45
11	U	H	2
12	U	H	24

Notes

1. U = Unvulcanized V = Vulcanized
2. T = Tensile strength. This is measured in MN/m^2
3. H = Hardness. This is a number measured on the hardness machine. A hard material has a high number.

Report to the boss

property	unit	unvulcanized	vulcanized
average value of tensile strength	MN/m^2		
average value of hardness	hardness number		

Strength and shape

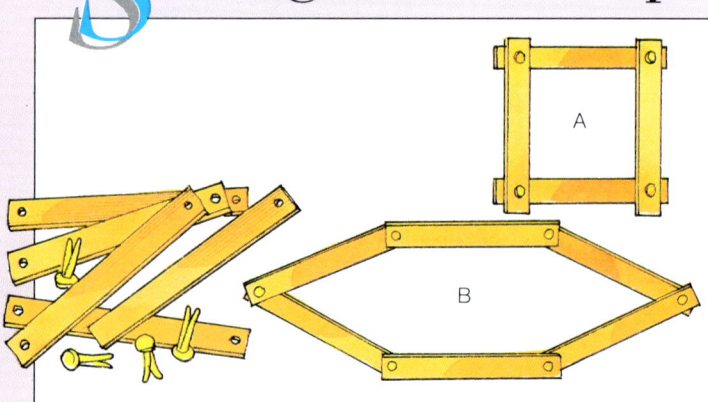

Finding a strong shape for a framework

BMX bike

Frameworks using triangles for strength

A roof made from corrugated plastic sheeting

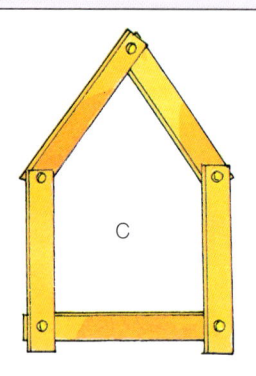

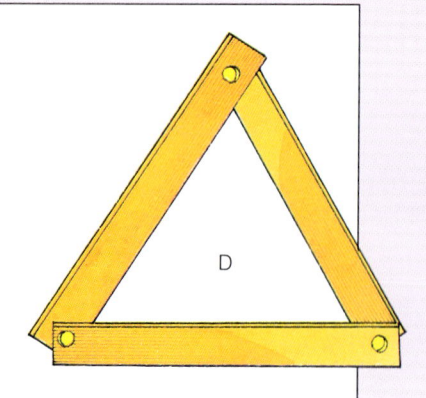

Shaping up

Cranes, bridges, electricity pylons, and house roofs are all examples of **frameworks**. A framework is a shape made from bars joined together. To be useful, a framework should be able to support both itself and some other load without falling down.

You can do some simple experiments on frameworks by loosely joining strips of cardboard with pins as shown. You will find that the only structure that will hold itself up and support any weight is a triangle. A triangular framework is a very strong shape. Other frameworks can be made strong by dividing them into triangles. Two different examples of frameworks which use triangles for strength are also shown.

1 Copy the photograph of a roof truss and colour in all the triangles you can find in it.

2 Redraw **A**, **B** and **C** from the top of the page adding extra strips inside the frameworks to make them strong.

3 What makes the BMX bike so strong?

4 From books and pamphlets supplied by your teacher find as many examples as you can of triangles being used to strengthen structures.

Corrugations

Sheets of material can be given extra strength by folding the material into **corrugations**. The photograph shows corrugated plastic sheeting being used as the roof of a summer house.

5 Give 1 other example of corrugation being used to give strength to a sheet of material.

6 Explain in your own words why corrugation works. (Hint: triangles.)

Even stronger!

Tubes

Frameworks are often built from **tubes** rather than solid bars. A tube is stronger than a solid bar of the same weight. A tube is another example of a strong shape. Look at part of the Forth Railway Bridge. Many of the triangular shaped frameworks have been made from tubes. This makes the bridge strong without making it too heavy. Tubes are also found in nature where strength and light weight are important. An example is a plant with a hollow stem.

1 Trace the photograph of the Forth Bridge and colour in the parts made from tubes.

2 Give 2 other examples of strong tubes found in nature.

Strong building blocks

If you take a wooden stick and bend it in the middle until it breaks you will see quite clearly from the splinters that the wood at the bottom has been torn apart. Although it is not so easy to see, the wood at the top has been squashed.

When concrete, wood, or steel beams are used for building they all bend slightly even if they are only supporting their own weight! They must be designed to stand up to this strain at the top and bottom.

The strength of a building beam also depends on which way up it is used.

Steel beams used for building are often made in the shape of a letter 'I'. This shape is deep for strength yet strengthened at the top and bottom where the strains are. An I-beam is strong and light. Concrete is a very useful material often used for building. However, it has a weakness. While it can take a lot of squeezing, it does not like being stretched. To make concrete beams stronger they are often **reinforced** (made stronger) by thin steel rods which are added to the parts likely to get stretched.

3 Explain in your words why an I-beam is strong.

Wood bent until broken   *An I-beam*

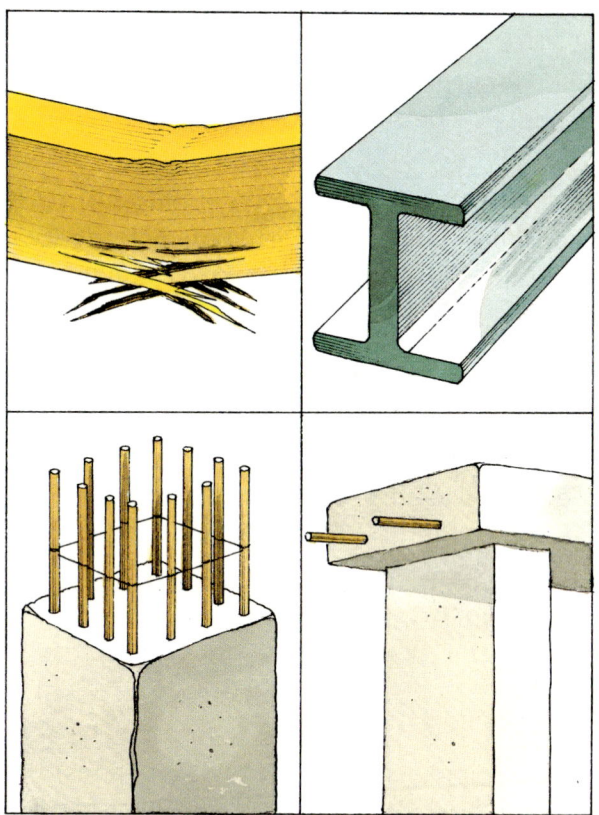

Concrete is re-inforced by steel rods

4 Why are the wooden planks used to hold up the floor in a house always used edge-on?

5 Look at the re-inforced concrete shapes. Why is the horizontal beam re-inforced only at the bottom while the vertical post is re-inforced all round the outside? (Hint: think where the stretching happens.)

Flammability

PETROL TANKER TRAGEDY

Catching fire

Materials which burn easily are said to be **flammable**. Some materials such as petrol burn so easily they cause explosions when set alight, often with disastrous results. Special safety precautions have to be taken when handling petrol.

Wood, too, burns easily. Large areas of forest are a special fire risk. Often when walking through forest land you will come across fire-fighting equipment.

1 What precautions against fire are taken at self-service petrol pumps?

2 Why are large areas of forest often broken up by clear spaces as shown in the photograph?

Fire and fashion

If you look at the table you will see that cotton catches fire and burns easily. Although cotton is comfortable to wear next to the skin, its **flammability** makes cotton pyjamas, night-dresses, and dressing gowns a fire risk.

Manufacturers worry about the flammability of night-clothes more than about normal day clothes because loose-fitting night-clothes can more easily touch a flame and, once alight, the material burns quickly due to the large amount of air on **both** sides of it.

Many night-clothes are **flame-proofed**. That is, they have been treated with special chemicals to stop them burning so easily. They often carry a special label to let you know this. Sometimes washing removes the flame-proofing and the label will warn you if this is the case.

3 Give 2 reasons why a man's woollen suit is less of a fire-risk than a lady's cotton night-dress.

Flame-proofing

The table opposite shows the results of a test that was carried out to find what effect flame-proofing had on 4 different fabrics. Each number shown is the total burning time from first touching the flame until burning ended.

4 Which is the most flammable before flame-proofing?

5 Before flame-proofing which material burns most slowly?

6 Which material is least affected by flame-proofing?

7 Which material burned most slowly once flame-proofed?

8 Which material should not be chosen to make a night-dress?

Material	How it behaves in a flame	out of a flame
Cotton	burns quickly with yellow flame	continues to burn
Wool	smoulders	goes out
Nylon	melts and burns with difficulty	goes out
Polyester	melts and shrinks from flame. Makes flame sooty	goes out

Comparing how different fabrics burn

Why are trees planted with regular gaps in between

Fabric	Time to burn. No flame-proofing. seconds	Time to burn. With flame-proofing. seconds
Wool	20	150
Cotton	10	50
Nylon	30	45
Polyester	15	35

Comparing the effect of flameproofing on 4 different fabrics

Lavoisier

Dear Ortlieb,

Tomorrow I am to be tried by the Revolutionary Tribunal and perhaps executed. The thought of facing 'Madame La Guillotine' fills me with dread. The Tribunal will see me only as a hated tax collector and a member of the nobility but I will argue that I have given much to the people. What could be more precious than scientific knowledge!

It was once believed that all things contained a mysterious substance called 'phlogiston'. When things burned the phlogiston escaped and the flame was the escaping phlogiston. Stuff and nonsense! If this were true then substances would lose weight when they burn. I showed that they gained weight. My experiments showed that when substances burn they join with a gas which is contained in the air all around us. This gas I have named oxygen. I am convinced that when something burns it joins very rapidly with the oxygen in the air. The flame seen during burning is simply the burning of the gases which are driven off by the heat.

To test the idea that burning needs oxygen I have tried heating sulphur in a jar containing no air whatsoever. It did not burn. Yet when I heated it in a jar full of oxygen it burned very quickly.

I am convinced my discoveries will open the door to a new understanding of science. Surely the people owe me a great debt.

Yours in despair,

Antoine Lavoisier

Lavoisier using the apparatus to investigate burning

On May 8th 1794, after a very short trial, Lavoisier was guillotined. Joseph Lagrange, a great mathematician of the time, remarked "It required only a moment to sever that head, and perhaps a century will not be sufficient to produce another like it"

A foam extinguisher putting out a fire

1 What is the above piece of writing about:
  a The French Revolution
  b Oxygen
  c What happens when something burns?

2 By using the index of this book find what percentage of oxygen is contained in the air.

3 What is a flame?

4 Air is a mixture of gases. Which one is needed to allow things to burn?

5 What important discovery did Lavoisier make which showed that a flame was not 'escaping phlogiston'?

6 What experiment did Lavoisier do which showed that air was needed for burning?

7 Look at the photograph of a modern foam fire extinguisher. Explain how this puts out fires.

8 Lavoisier also tried heating a mixture of sulphur and saltpetre in a gas jar with no air. This time it did burn. Can you suggest why?

Dangerous stuff

Safe as houses?

We all like to think of our home as a safe place to live. It comes as a shock to find that using household materials wrongly could lead to death or injury by burning, explosion, poisoning, or skin damage.

Fumes

Substances used for painting, decorating, cleaning, and repairing often contain petrol-like chemicals which give off **dangerous fumes**. These fumes may be **highly flammable** or **poisonous**, or both. Often the label carries a warning 'Not to be used in a confined space'. This means it should only be used where there is plenty of moving air to stop the fumes building up.

Glue sniffers get high by deliberately breathing the poisonous fumes which come from certain glues. This damages their bodies so much that some of them die.

Poisons

Young children will pop almost anything into their mouths. Medicines which are quite safe for adults can poison children and should be kept in special **child-proof containers**.

Corrosive substances

A corrosive substance is one that will chemically burn anything it touches including skin. An **irritant** such as fibre-glass wool irritates the skin and can cause skin complaints if it is not handled with protective gloves. Some irritants can also damage the lungs if breathed in.

Radioactivity

Radioactive substances give off invisible but harmful rays. Such substances should always be carefully stored in lead-lined containers, marked with a special sign. Although radioactive substances are not commonly found in the home, certain types of smoke detectors use radioactive substances to detect particles of smoke.

Aerosols

Aerosol cans contain substances mixed with gas under pressure. If they are punctured or heated they can explode **even if the substance inside is non-flammable**.

1 List 5 dangerous materials which can sometimes be found in the home and write a short sentence about each.

Play it safe — read the label

GUN SIEGE BOYS HAD BEEN SNIFFING GLUE

Three boys who had been sniffing glue fired air rifles, shot guns and .22 rifles wildly causing damage estimated at tens of thousands of pounds during a siege lasting more than six hours at a gun shop.

The Lord Justice Clerk said The fact that you were sniffing glue is no excuse in the eyes of the law.

Two of the boys were given a sentence of three years and the other will be sentenced next week.

Shaving foam. Safe or dangerous?

Avoiding danger

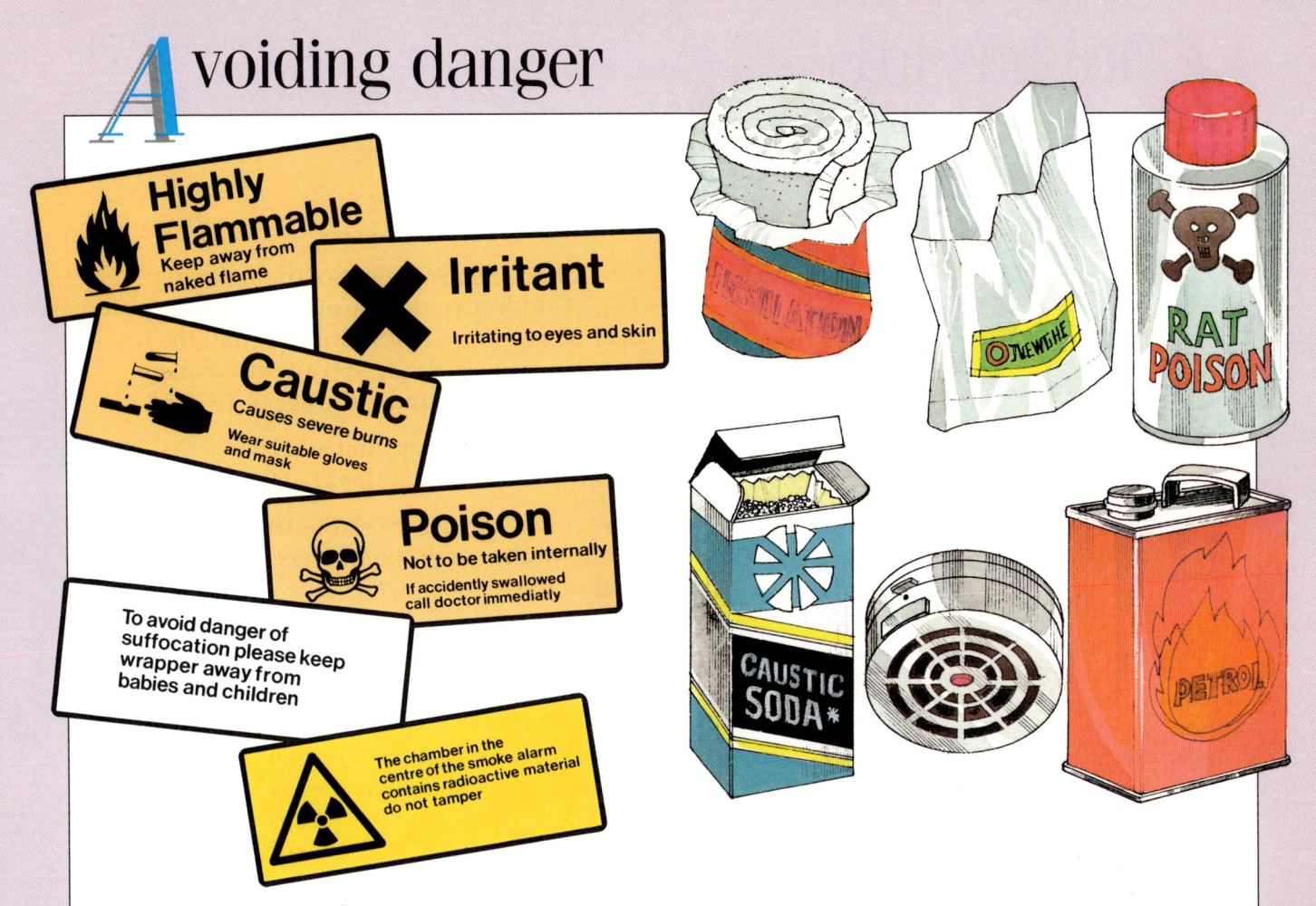

Warning labels

Dangerous substances

1. Match the labels on the left with the objects on the right.

2. Draw the symbols which are used to show danger due to:
   a flammability
   b radio-activity
   c corrosive substance
   d irritant
   e poison.

3. The warning shown opposite appeared on the aerosol tin of a substance used for sealing holes. Describe in your own words the dangers of using the substance.

4. Look at the part of the index for a book about housekeeping.
   a Which pages would you look up to find a safe way of storing flammable substances?
   b A person in your family has accidently swallowed some bleach. Which *two* parts of the book would you look up while waiting for the doctor to arrive?
   c Your friend says it is perfectly safe to throw a used aerosol tin of spray paint into a fire. You are not so sure. Where might you find advice in this book?

CAUTION

Pressurised container.

Protect from sunlight and do not expose to temperatures greater than 50°C.

Do not pierce or burn even after use.

Do not spray on a naked flame.

Use in a well-ventilated place.

Avoid breathing the vapour.

Keep out of the reach of children.

Not for use with polystyrene or fibreglass.

A warning on an aerosol tin

Acetate	140 141	Heating	72
Aerosols	99 101	Irons	225
Asbestos	131	Kitchens	205
Bedmaking	31	Jute	26
Boilers	103 104	Paint	232
Carpets	23, 57	Poisions	56
Chairs	89 90	Polish	64 67
Decorating	77	Refrigerators	94 98
First aid	3, 4	Sheets	60
Glass	58, 59	Storage	207

Part of the index from a housekeeping book

Fire hazard

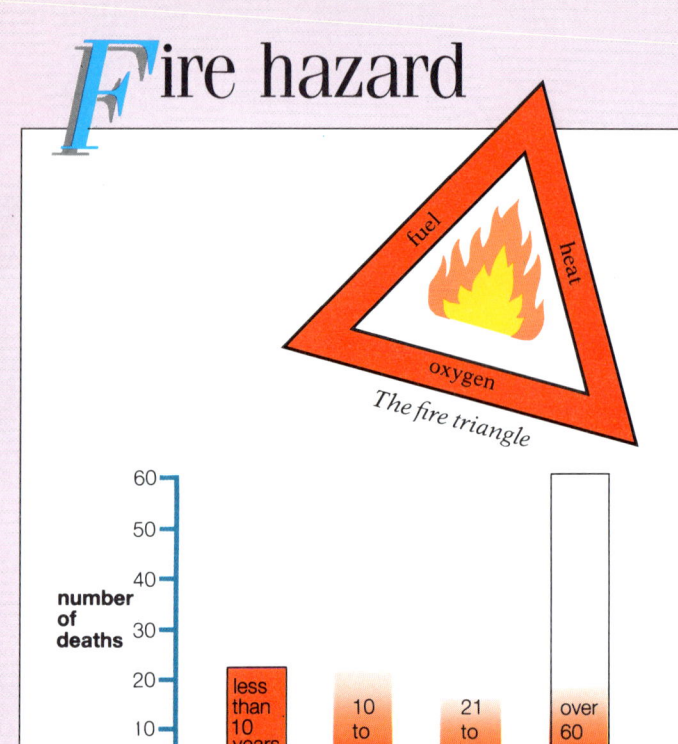

The fire triangle

Fire deaths in Scotland in one year

A fire-resistant suit protects from heat and flames

A fireman uses a breathing set to enter a smoke-filled building

Fire deaths

Fire killed 155 people in Scotland during 1983. Children under the age of 10 and people over 60 accounted for more than half the total but 58 people in the 21–60 age group also died. 22 children under the age of 10 died.

1 Copy the bar chart and add the information about the 21–60 age range.

2 *Estimate* the deaths in the 10–20 age range and in the over 60 age range and complete the chart.

Smoke, the killer

A fire starts as a result of three things coming together, **heat**, **fuel**, and **oxygen**. These three are sometimes shown as the **fire triangle**. Each or all of these three things can play their part in causing a fire death.

The tremendous amount of heat created in a fire can burn a victim to death. Special clothing is often worn by fire-fighters to protect them from the heat and flames. Usually in a fire the victim does not die from the heat but from breathing the smoke. Many household materials which are normally quite safe give off dangerous fumes in the heat of a fire. Examples are polyurethane foam found in easy chairs, PVC, a common plastic, and rubber also common in the house. In a fire the fumes from all these can cause death.

As the fire burns, oxygen is used up and carbon dioxide is produced. The carbon dioxide causes the fire-victim to breathe quickly and so take in more of the deadly smoke. The lack of oxygen can also cause death. A handkerchief placed across the mouth and nose like you see in the films does not protect you from the poisonous gases nor does it do anything about the lack of oxygen. A fireman entering a burning building where there is a lot of smoke carries his own fresh air with him.

3 Name 3 ways death can be caused in a fire.

4 Name another way in which smoke could cause death in a fire.

Poisonous gases

Death by poison gas

The intense heat of a house fire can make household materials give off poisonous gases.

Burning wool and silk can release the poisonous gas hydrogen cyanide. This is the same gas used in some American states to execute criminals in the gas chamber. Polyurethane foam, a foam plastic widely used in plastic cushions and household furniture, releases hydrogen cyanide when burning and can cause death in seconds. A careless cigarette left smouldering on a sofa or mattress filled with this foam can cause death by poison gas even without a fire.

Another plastic, PVC (polyvinyl chloride), breaks down at high temperatures to produce deadly hydrogen chloride. Burning rubber produces a poisonous mixture of sulphur dioxide and hydrogen sulphide. This mixture is particularly deadly because sulphur dioxide is heavier than air and sinks to the floor.

When materials which contain carbon burn, the carbon joins with the oxygen in the air to form carbon dioxide. Large amounts can kill. Small amounts make you breathe faster.

When most of the oxygen has been used up in the fire then carbon monoxide is produced instead of carbon dioxide.

Experts on fires have discovered that most people killed by house fires could not find their way out because of the smoke and were then either suffocated by lack of oxygen or poisoned by carbon monoxide.

Carbon monoxide poisoning

In your bloodstream there are many red blood cells which carry oxgyen around your body. When you breathe in carbon monoxide, during a fire for example, the carbon monoxide stops the red cells from doing their proper job of carrying oxgyen. When about 2/3 of the red cells are busy carrying carbon monoxide instead of oxygen you die from lack of oxygen in the body.

Burning or smouldering furniture can give off poisonous fumes

1. If there is time close doors and windows behind you
2. Each person should know at least two ways out from any room in the house
3. If the smoke is heavy crawl along the floor and try not to breath deeply
4. Never open a door which feels hot or is leaking smoke
5. Get out quickly
6. Phone for the Fire Brigade from a safe distance

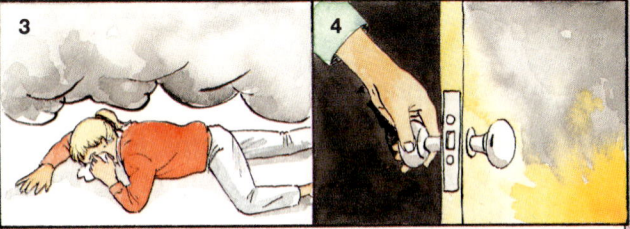

What to do in a fire

1. Look at each of the above pictures in turn and explain why the captions make good sense.
2. Why would the suggestion in picture 3 not work very well if there was a lot of burning rubber in the house?

27

Damage and protection

Cushioning the blow

Every day the Post Office in Britain handles about 600 000 parcels. You may have seen inside a sorting office and noticed that parcels are often quite roughly treated. They are bumped along conveyor belts and thrown onto piles of other parcels. This may damage the contents of the parcels unless they are properly protected against the bumps. Some ways of doing this are shown opposite.

Expanded polystyrene foam can be shaped to fit the object exactly and so cushion it from bumps. Sometimes polystyrene chips are used to surround the object. Straw is less common nowadays and is only occasionally found in parcels. It has been replaced by shredded paper.

A very useful type of packing is a thin plastic sheet containing hundreds of air bubbles. Because air is soft and springy the sheet cushions the object it is wrapped around. This type of plastic sheet is used inside padded envelopes.

Protecting fabrics

Fabrics used for clothes, curtains, and furniture can be damaged in many different ways. Apart from being rubbed or torn they may also be damaged by fire or water, eaten by moths, or ruined by incorrect washing and ironing. Sometimes a fabric is 'proofed', that is, treated with special protective chemicals. **Fire-proofing** makes it less easy to burn. **Water-proofing** stops water from getting into the fabric while **moth-proofing** makes the fabric indigestible so that the moth grub dies from lack of food.

Fabrics which have been proofed usually carry a special label telling you how to treat them so that you do not destroy the proofing.

Special-care labels on clothes also tell you the correct way to wash and iron them so that you do not damage the material through too much heat while washing or ironing. One system of labelling is shown.

Bubble packing

Good packing protects against damage

treatment	minimum precaution necessary	some caution necessary	special care necessary	treatment prohibited
washing	95	60	30	✗
bleaching (with chlorine)	Cl			✗
ironing	•••	••	•	✗

washing
The figure shown in the washtub symbol is the temperature of the water in degrees Celcius

ironing
The dots show the temperature of the iron
1 Dot • cool iron
2 Dots •• warm iron
3 Dots ••• hot iron

Care-labelling

1 Cotton needs a hot iron. Silk needs a warm iron. Polyester needs a cool iron. What kind of scarf would have a label with [iron symbol]?

2 What does the symbol [crossed-out symbol] mean on a garment?

3 What label would you expect to find on a very delicate fabric which needed a cool wash and could not be ironed?

Dry rot

A lot of rot

Dry wood lasts a long time but wet wood can be damaged by **rotting**. Rotting is caused by a fungus, that is, a plant related to a mushroom. A fungus produces millions of **spores** which float through the air to land on wood. If the wood is wet enough the spores produce fungus which feeds on the wood and breaks it down.

These wood-destroying spores are around us all the time but they only take a hold if wood becomes very damp. One common type of rot is called **dry rot** because once the wood has rotted it looks like a dry powder.

1 What two things must be present for dry rot to start?

2 Explain in your own words how dry rot spreads.

Stopping the rot

To prevent wood rotting it is important to stop water getting into the wood. One common way of doing this is to make the wood waterproof by covering it with several coats of paint. For wood which is outdoors this has to be repeated every few years as the paint gets chipped and cracked due to the effects of the sun, rain, and frost.

A **damp-proof course** is a waterproof barrier at the foot of a brick wall. It stops water seeping up the bricks in the wall and rotting the wooden timbers inside a house. The damp-proof course is built into the wall by the brick-layers when the house is being built.

Special air-holes are built into houses to allow air to circulate under the floors and so keep the timbers dry. In kitchens and bathrooms, where lots of water splashes about, special sealing substances are used to stop water dropping through cracks onto the floor boards.

3 List four ways of preventing dry rot in houses and write a sentence about each one.

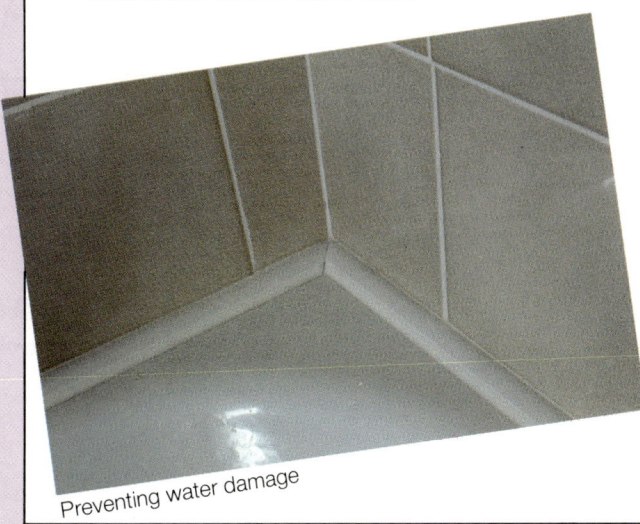

Dry rot

Wood can be protected by painting it

A damp-proof course stops rising damp

Preventing water damage

Air holes allows air to circulate

Metal corrosion

Corrosion

Some metals **corrode** when they are left without a protective covering. A metal corrodes by slowly changing into a new substance while the original metal gets eaten away.

When iron corrodes the iron slowly joins with the oxygen in the air and changes to **iron oxide** or **rust**. Although paint can keep out the oxygen and water needed to let the metal rust, once the paint is scratched rust can form very quickly as every car-owner knows!

Copper also corrodes when left exposed to the weather. Rain and chemicals dissolved in the rain-water change the surface of the copper to **copper carbonate** or **verdigris**. You may have seen the bright green colour of verdigris on a copper roof.

Two other metals, aluminium and zinc, join very quickly with the oxygen in the air. They become covered all over with oxide. However, in their case the oxide protects them from further corrosion. For this reason aluminium and zinc are often used for jobs where corrosion would be a nuisance. For example zinc is sometimes used to form water-tight joints on roofs.

Rust

Verdigris

Zinc Joints

An experiment with rust

When curious Kate asked her science teacher why her Dad's car was always rusting she was given an experiment to do. She cleaned 4 iron nails and put them into 4 different test tubes filled with 4 different things. She left them for a week and then came back to look at them.

Look at the page from her laboratory notebook then answer the following questions.

1 Which nails did not rust at all?

2 Why did Kate put oil on the top of the 'oxygen free' water?

3 Which nail rusts the most?

4 Which 2 substances are needed for iron to rust?

5 In winter salt is used to melt the snow on the roads. What effect does this have on motor cars using the road?

6 How did Kate explain to her Dad why his car was always rusting?

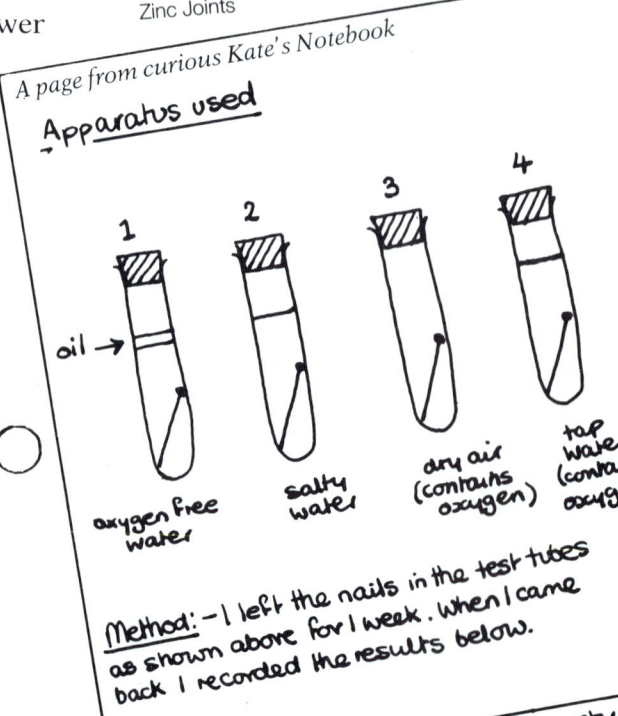

Protection against corrosion

Anodising

Aluminium can be forced to grow a thicker oxide layer by a special process called anodising. The protective layer of oxide can be dyed various colours to give the metal a very attractive appearance. The photograph shows part of anodised bicycle.

Anodising protects the surface of aluminium

Electro-plating

Electro-plating is a way of giving a metal object a protective covering of another metal. It is done in a special bath using electricity. Look at an object being copper plated. When the electric current flows small particles of copper move towards the object and stick to it. At the same time the lump of copper loses some copper.

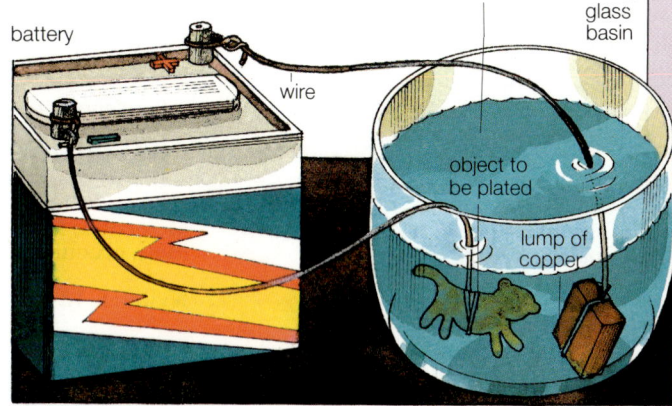

Electroplating puts a thin protective layer of metal on the surface

Galvanising

Galvanising is a way of protecting the surface of steel from corrosion. By dipping the steel into hot molten zinc the steel is given a protective coat of zinc. Some galvanised objects are shown in the photograph.

These steel objects have all been galvanised

Physical and chemical protection of metals

Metal will not corrode if air and water are kept away from the surface of the metal. So one way of stopping corrosion is to paint the metal surface or cover it with a thin layer of protecting metal as in electro-plating. Painting and electro-plating are examples of **physical protection**. If the surface layer is scratched the metal underneath will corrode.

Chemical protection is another way to stop metals corroding. Sometimes when two different metals touch each other an unusual chemical reaction happens which allows one metal to corrode but not the other. Galvanising is a good example of chemical protection. The steel does not rust even when the zinc is scratched. Unfortunately zinc is poisonous so galvanised steel containers can't be used for food.

1 List four different ways of protecting metal against corrosion.

2 State whether the following are examples of physical or chemical protection: painting, anodising, electro-plating, galvanising.

3 'Tin cans' are made from steel covered with a layer of tin. They rust easily when scratched. Is the steel chemically or physically protected?

4 Oil rigs often have big lumps of magnesium attached to the submerged legs. Suggest why.

Index

Aggregate, 7
Air
   as a heat insulator, 13
   bubbles, protection by, 28
   vent, 29
Alloy, 6, 16
Aluminium, 12, 14, 30, 31
Anodising, 31

Blood cells, 27
Bridges, 12, 21
Bronze, 6
Burning, 22, 23

Cables, copper, 12
Cancer, 14
Cans, tin, 31
Carbon, 16
Carbon dioxide, 26, 27
Carbon monoxide, 27
Chemical protection of metals, 31
Clothes, 4, 8, 13, 14, 15
Concrete, 7, 9, 21
Conductor of electricity, 10, 12
Copper, 5, 6, 12, 30
Corrosion, 24, 30, 31
Cotton, 8

Damp-proof course, 29
Death by fire, 26
Diamond, 9
Dry rot, 29
Dyeing, 15

Electrical, conductivity of
   materials, 10
Electricity, 10, 12
Electroplating, 31
Elastic, 19
Element, 16
Extinguisher, fire, 23

Fabric, 13
   flame testing a, 10
   proofing of, 28
   wear resistance of, 10
Fibre optics, 13
Fibres,
   natural and man-made, 8, 13
Fire, 22, 23, 26, 27
Flame, 23
   testing, 10
   proofing, 22
Fumes, 24, 26, 27
Furnace, smelting, 16

Galvanizing, 31
Gas, poisonous, 26, 27
Glue,
   sniffing, 24
   testing of, 11

Heat
   good conductor of, 9
   resistant, 9, 11
House fires, 26, 27
Household, materials, 24, 25
Hydrogen chloride, 27

I-beam, 21
Insulator, 11, 12
Investigating
   rusting, 30
   strength of glue, 11
   thermal conductivity, 10, 11
Iron, 16
   oxide, 30
Irritant, 24, 25

Labels, clothes, 8
Laser, 13
Lavoisier, 23

Macintosh, 15
Materials, 14
   electrical conductivity of, 10
   hardness of, 9, 19
   household, dangers from, 24
   natural, 4
   properties of, 9
   thermal conductivity of, 10
Metals, 12
Molecules, 18
Moth proofing, 28

Nylon, 5, 12, 18

Oil rigs, protection of, 31
Ores, 6, 16
Oxide, iron, 30
Oxygen, 23
   lack of, 26

Painting, waterproofing by, 29
Petrol, fire risk from, 22
Poisonous fumes, 24, 26, 27
Polymer, 18
Polystyrene, 5, 12, 14, 18, 28
Plastic, 12, 18
Protection of metals, 31
PVC, 9, 12, 26, 27

Red blood cells, 27
Roof, 20
   water-tight joints on, 30
Rope, 13
Rotting, 29
Rubber, 9, 15, 19, 26, 27
Rust, 30

Silicon chip, 12
Smelting, 6, 16
Smoke
   deadly effects of, 26
   detector, 24
Sniffing glue, 24
Stainless steel, 17
Steel, 5, 6, 9, 12, 16, 17, 21
Stone, 4
Suffocation, 27
Sulphur dioxide, 27
Suspension bridges, 12, 17

Tensile strength, 18
Thermal conductivity, 10, 11
Thermoplastic, 18
Tools, 4, 6
Triangles, as strong shapes, 20
Tubes for strength, 21

Waterproof, 9, 15
Waterproofing
   of fabrics, 28
   of houses, 29
Wear resistance of a fabric, 10
Wood, 4, 6, 8, 22, 29
Wool, fumes from burning, 27

Zinc, oxide, 30